Carly Patterson

By Jeff Savage

AMAZING ATHLETES

Lerner Publications Company • Minneapolis

This book is available in two editions:
Library binding by Lerner Publications Company
   A division of Lerner Publishing Group, Inc.
Soft cover by First Avenue Editions
   An imprint of Lerner Publishing Group, Inc.
241 First Avenue North
Minneapolis, MN 55401 U.S.A.

Website address: www.lernerbooks.com

Library of Congress Cataloging-in-Publication Data

Savage, Jeff, 1961–
     Carly Patterson / by Jeff Savage.
        p.   cm. — (Amazing athletes)
     Includes index.
     ISBN-13: 978–0–8225–2639–1 (lib. bdg. : alk. paper)
     ISBN-10: 0–8225–2639–5 (lib. bdg. : alk. paper)
     ISBN-13: 978–0–8225–2640–7 (pbk. : alk. paper)
     ISBN-10: 0–8225–2640–9 (pbk. : alk. paper)
     1. Patterson, Carly, 1988– Juvenile literature. 2. Gymnasts—United States—Biography—Juvenile literature. I. Title. II. Series.
     GV460.2.P25S38 2005
     796.44'092—dc22   2004028211

Manufactured in the United States of America
3 4 5 6 7 8 – DP – 13 12 11 10 09 08

TABLE OF CONTENTS

Carly stays focused as she performs on the balance beam at the 2004 Olympic Games in Athens, Greece.

Going for Gold

Carly Patterson stood barefoot on the **balance** beam. She smiled, and the sparkles in her red **leotard** flashed brightly. Carly was competing against 23 other gymnasts in the **all-around** competition at the 2004 Olympic Games in Athens, Greece. The crowd at the Olympic Indoor Hall was watching her every move. Millions of people around the world were tuned in on television. This was the biggest contest of Carly's life.

Gymnastics features team and individual events. The greatest individual competition is the all-around. The women's all-around is made up of four events. They are the vault, uneven bars, balance beam, and floor exercise.

Carly performs a cartwheel on the balance beam.

Carly looked straight ahead and began her **routine.** She twirled and flipped along the four-inch-wide beam. Carly stands just five feet tall. She weighs 99 pounds. But she looked as light as a feather on the beam.

Carly performed **aerials** and graceful dance moves. After each move, she landed silently on the beam. She was careful not to wobble or slip. Any mistakes would hurt her **score.**

Carly set up her **dismount** with a difficult and dangerous series of handsprings. This gave her extra power to jump high off the end of the beam. She did a half twist and then two quick flips through the air. She landed flat on her feet. It was a super routine!

Carly smiles and raises her arms after performing a perfect dismount.

Carly gives her coach, Evgeny Marchenko, a big hug after her great performance.

The crowd cheered. Carly smiled and waved. Then she ran and hugged her coach, Evgeny Marchenko. They both watched the scoreboard. What would her score be?

Carly stood in fourth place. She needed a good score to stay in the hunt for the gold medal. The judges posted the number on the board—9.725. A very good score! Carly's name moved to the top of the board. She was in the lead for the **gold medal!**

Carly and her coach giggled. Only one **event** remained—the floor exercise. Could she keep her lead over Russian superstar Svetlana Khorkina? Would any of the other gymnasts be able to catch her? Could Carly's gold medal dream come true?

Carly's hometown, Baton Rouge, is the capital of Louisiana.

DISCOVERING THE SPORT

Carly Rae Patterson was born February 4, 1988, to Natalie and Ricky Patterson. Carly and her younger sister, Jordan, lived with their parents in Baton Rouge, Louisiana.

Carly discovered gymnastics when she was six years old. One day, she went to a birthday party that was being held at a gym. She and the other kids played on the **tumbling mats.** After watching some older girls do tricks, Carly tried her first flip. It did not work. But Carly realized that gymnastics was fun.

A few days later, Carly was home in her backyard. She was trying to teach herself how to do a **back walkover.** Carly put her hands above her head and leaned backward. She kept her head back. She set her hands firmly on the ground. Carly tried to push her feet up and back. After many tries, she began to learn the move.

To reach her goals, Carly had to go without a lot of things. For example, Carly avoids junk food to stay in shape. She only eats certain foods, such as chicken, fish, vegetables, fruit, yogurt, and granola.

Carly's hero is 1984 Olympic champion Mary Lou Retton. Retton was the first U.S. gymnast to win the gold medal in the all-around competition.

Later, Carly showed off her new skill to her mother. "Mom," she shouted, "look what I did!" Carly's mother gave her a worried look. "You are going to hurt yourself!" said Natalie. Carly's mom had practiced gymnastics as a child. She knew Carly needed proper training to keep from getting hurt. The next day, Natalie signed Carly up for a gymnastics class.

In class, Carly learned basic **tumbling** tricks. Soon she was competing in her first gymnastics **meet.** She finished in 13th place. Carly kept practicing. She improved quickly. At the age of seven, she was good enough to enter the U.S. Junior Olympics. Carly competed against other gymnasts her age from across the country. "Until that day," Carly said, "I thought I was really good." But she soon learned that she had a long way to go to be the best. She finished in 76th place.

U.S. gymnast Kerri Strug became a hero when she helped her team win the gold medal at the 1996 Olympic Games. She performed on a badly injured leg.

LEARNING COOL TRICKS

Carly was determined to get better. She kept practicing. She practiced in gymnastics class, at the gym, and in her backyard.

In the summer of 1996, Carly was outside working on a move when her mom called her into the living room. The women's gymnastics competition at the Olympic Games in Atlanta, Georgia, was playing on TV. Carly came in just in time to see U.S. gymnast Kerri Strug perform an excellent routine on the vault. Her performance won the gold medal for the United States in the **team competition.** Amazingly, Strug had performed on a badly injured ankle.

Carly watched as the U.S. coach carried the young gymnast to the **medal stand.** Carly was impressed with Strug's courage. "Awesome," Carly thought to herself.

That same year, the Patterson family moved to Allen, Texas. This turned out to be a lucky break for Carly. The World Olympic Gymnastics Academy was nearby in Plano, Texas. She joined the academy to work on her skills with some of the world's best gymnastics coaches.

Coach Evgeny Marchenko worked at the school. Marchenko quickly saw that Carly had natural talent. But she had a lot to learn. Carly did not know many of the basics. For example, she didn't know how to point her toes or keep her knees straight during routines. Doing these little things right are a key to earning good scores. "I had bad form. Bad everything," Carly admitted. But she worked hard and improved quickly. She soon became one of the academy's top gymnasts.

Carly learned many of her skills at the World Olympic Gymnastics Academy.

By 2000, 12-year-old Carly was ready to compete in her first **international** meet. She performed in the junior division of the Top Gym Tournament in Belgium. Carly won the **bronze medal** on the balance beam and the **silver medal** in all-around.

The next year, she won the gold medal in the all-around at the American Team Cup. Carly's hard work had really paid off. She was one of the best gymnasts in the country.

But Carly stumbled the next year. At the age of 13, she was competing at the Goodwill Games in Australia. She started out well. She went into the last event with the lead. But Carly performed badly in the floor exercise. She fell twice and finished in seventh place.

Carly works very hard to
be the best.

MAKING THE GRADE

Carly's setback at the Goodwill Games didn't
stop her from trying to get better. She kept
working hard. Carly trained for six hours a day.
She woke up at 5:45 every morning and
headed straight to the gym. She practiced for
three hours before school. After school was
over, Carly practiced gymnastics for another
three hours.

Meanwhile, Carly kept competing in meets. The trophy case in her bedroom filled up with awards and trophies. By the age of 15, she was one of the world's top gymnasts.

But Carly isn't just talented. She is also tough. She showed her toughness at the 2003 World Championships. During practice, she landed badly on her arm. Her elbow swelled up. Coaches tried to treat the injury, but nothing really worked. Carly could not straighten her arm.

Still, she refused to let a doctor look at her arm. "I didn't want to find out what was wrong," she said. "I knew they would tell me not to compete." Even though she was hurt, Carly was determined to perform. Over the next two days, she helped lead the U.S. team to the gold medal.

Later, Carly competed in the all-around competition. She just barely missed winning the gold herself. She finished second to Russian champion Svetlana Khorkina by just 0.188 points. After the competition, Carly had her arm examined. It was broken. She immediately underwent three hours of surgery. She could not compete for the next three months.

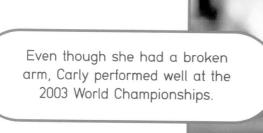

Even though she had a broken arm, Carly performed well at the 2003 World Championships.

Russian superstar Svetlana Khorkina (center) won the gold medal at the 2003 World Championships. Carly finished second to win the silver. Chinese gymnast Nan Zhang (left) finished third and won the bronze.

Once her arm healed, Carly went back to training at full steam. She wanted to compete in the biggest event in gymnastics, the Olympic Games in 2004. The whole world would be watching.

Carly performs a routine on the uneven bars at the 2004 Olympic Games.

GOLDEN GIRL OF GYMNASTICS

By the summer of 2004, Carly was feeling great. She easily made the U.S. Women's Olympic Gymnastics Team. As a member of Team USA, Carly was living a dream. She was competing for her country in the world's biggest sporting event. Millions of television viewers would be watching.

The team competition came first. Team USA was a **favorite** to win the gold medal. But they were up against some great gymnasts from China, Romania, Russia, and other countries.

Team USA would have to be almost perfect to win. But Carly's teammate Courtney Kupets struggled in the floor exercise. Then Carly struck the bar with her foot during her routine on the uneven bars. Her mistake cost the team some important points. In the end, Team USA made too many mistakes. They finished second, winning the silver medal. Romania won the gold.

Coach Evgeny Marchenko talks to Carly after a poor routine on the uneven bars.

Next, everyone looked to Carly as the United States' brightest hope in the all-around. Carly's first event was the vault. She ran down the runway and vaulted high in the air. But she landed crookedly and just out of bounds. Because of her mistake, the judges gave her a poor score—9.375. This put Carly in eighth place.

Carly makes a strong vault during the all-around competition. But she landed poorly and lost points.

ATHENS 2004

Carly had to do better in her second event, the uneven bars. She came through in a big way. Carly performed a strong routine. The judges gave her a 9.575. But Russian superstar Svetlana Khorkina scored better.

Carly was in fourth place with two events left. Next up was the balance beam. Carly nailed her routine to edge past Khorkina. Carly was in first place! Could she keep her lead?

The final event was the floor exercise. Several gymnasts took their turn before Carly. Khorkina performed a dazzling routine. She scored a 9.562.

Carly's turn was next. She needed a strong score to stay in first place. Millions of people were watching. Would she succeed? Carly had been working for this moment for years. She was confident. She believed in herself.

Teammate Courtney Kupets whispered in her ear, "Smile and have fun." Carly started her routine to the jazzy music. She made four **tumbling passes.** She jumped incredibly high. On her third tumbling pass, she did two somersaults in midair and landed perfectly. When she nailed her last pass, the crowd exploded with cheers. Carly had performed brilliantly!

Carly sprints forward to begin a tumbling pass during her floor exercise routine.

The judges posted her score. It was 9.712, better than anyone else's. Carly had won the gold medal! She leaped into the arms of coach Evgeny Marchenko and burst into tears of joy. Chants of "U-S-A, U-S-A" filled the arena. Fans waved U.S. flags. "I don't even know what to say right now," said Carly afterward. "It's just amazing. I hope this inspires every young girl to strive for her dreams."

But Carly still wasn't finished. Four nights later, she competed again on the balance beam. This time, she won a second silver medal.

Carly had won three medals! She was the new superstar of women's gymnastics. As the Patterson family packed up to fly back to the United States, Carly's mother offered to buy her daughter a souvenir bracelet or necklace. Carly smiled and shook her head no. Her gold medal hung from her neck. She rubbed it with her fingers. "This is all I wanted, right here," she said.

Carly shows off her gold medal. Svetlana Khorkina (left) won the silver. Nan Zhang finished third for the bronze.

Selected Career Highlights

2004 Won the gold medal in the all-around competition at the
Olympic Games
Helped the U.S. team win the silver medal at the
Olympic Games
Won the silver medal in the balance beam at the
Olympic Games
Won the gold medal in the all-around at the Visa
American Cup

2003 Won the gold medal in the all-around at the Visa
American Cup
Won the silver medal in the all-around at the World
Championships
Helped the U.S. team win the gold medal at the
World Championships

2002 Won the gold medal in the all-around at the Junior Nationals

2001 Won the gold medal in the all-around at the American Team Cup

2000 Won the silver medal in the all-around and the bronze medal in
the balance beam at the Top Gym Tournament in Belgium

Glossary

aerials: midair moves

all-around: an individual event in the women's competition in which
athletes compete on the vault, uneven bars, balance beam, and floor
exercise

back walkover: a tumbling move in which the gymnast arches backward,
touches the ground, and pulls her legs over her head one at a time

balance beam: an event during which the gymnast performs on the
balance beam. A balance beam is 4 inches wide and 16 feet long.

bronze medal: the medal given to the third-place finisher

dismount: jumping off the balance beam or uneven bars to end a routine

events: competitions to find out the best team or individual. Women's
gymnastics events include the vault, balance beam, uneven bars, and floor
exercise.

favorite: an athlete or a team that is expected to do well or to win

floor exercise: in gymnastics, an event in which the gymnast performs dance steps and tumbling moves to music on a 40-square-foot mat

gold medal: the medal awarded to the first-place finisher

international: made up of or including different countries from around the world

leotard: the skin-tight, one-piece uniform worn by gymnasts

medal stand: a platform on which winning athletes stand to receive their medals

meet: in gymnastics, a gathering where gymnasts compete against one another

routine: a planned series of steps, jumps, and other moves performed by gymnasts

score: in gymnastics, the number of points awarded for an athlete's performance. A group of judges gives a score for a routine. Good routines receive higher scores. The best score is a 10. The gymnast loses points each time a mistake is made.

silver medal: the medal given to the second-place finisher

team competition: in gymnastics, an event where teams of gymnasts compete. The team with the best overall score wins the event.

tumbling: performing flips and other moves on the mat

tumbling mats: padded mats used for practicing gymnastics moves

tumbling passes: in the floor exercise, the flips, somersaults, and other moves

uneven bars: an event in which the gymnast performs on a set of 8-foot-long bars. One bar is set 8 feet high. The second bar is set about $5\frac{1}{2}$ feet high.

vault: in gymnastics, an event in which the gymnast runs down a runway, jumps onto a springboard, pushes with her hands off the vault (also called a horse), and lands on a mat

Further Reading & Websites

Jensen, Julie. *Beginning Gymnastics*. Adapted from Linda Wallenberg Bragg's *Fundamental Gymnastics*. Minneapolis: Lerner Sports, 1995.

Gifford, Clive. *Summer Olympics: The Definitive Guide to the World's Greatest Sports Celebration*. Boston: Kingfisher, 2004.

Jackman, Joan. *Gymnastics*. New York: Dorling Kindersley Publishers, 2000.

Oxlade, Chris, and David Ballheimer. *Olympics*. New York: Dorling Kindersley Publishers, 1999.

Carly Patterson.org
http://www.carlypatterson.org
Carly's official website features photos and information about Carly and the sport of gymnastics.

Official USA Gymnastics Site
http://www.usa-gymnastics.org
The official USA Gymnastics website has biographies of athletes and information about events.

Sports Illustrated for Kids
http://www.sikids.com
The *Sports Illustrated for Kids* website covers all sports, including gymnastics.

Index

Photo Acknowledgments

Photographs are used with the permission of: © Icon SMI, pp. 4, 6, 22, 26, 28, 29; © Erich Schlegel/NewSport/Corbis, p. 7; © DYLAN MARTINEZ/Reuters/Corbis, p. 8; © Nik Wheeler/CORBIS, p. 10; © Neal Preston/CORBIS, p. 12; © E. SCHLEGEL/DALLAS MORNING NEWS/CORBIS SYGMA, p. 14; © Pizzazz Photo, pp. 16, 18; © Smiley N. Pool/Dallas Morning News/Corbis, pp. 23, 27; SportsChrome East/West, Michael Zito, p. 20; © Tom Theobald/ZUMA Press, p. 21; © Steven E. Sutton/Duomo/Corbis, p. 24.

Front Cover: © CNS/Imaginechina/ZUMA press